About the Author

Tatiana Semenova, practical psychologist, teacher of psychology, specialization – clinical psychology. Graduated from the Moscow Medical College №1, specializing in nursing. Generalist Nurse. I worked at the Scientific Research Institute of Transplantology and Artificial Organs, in the Department of Rhythm Disorders, Cardiac Surgery and Assisted Circulation. I have a diploma in therapeutic massage. Graduated from the Institute of Psychology and Pedagogy, Moscow. Completed practice in psychiatry, neurology, defectology, in state institutions in Moscow. Internship at a public and private school in the Moscow region.

Marital status: married; family: two children. I am engaged in the study of psychological, social problems and ways to solve them. Throughout this time, a lot of interesting information was collected, which later became the reason to write a book about isolation in the aspects of family, age, and clinical, social psychology.

I hope you will find in this publication useful information about the impact of quarantine on the psychological aspects of each of us. The author personally went through a series of described events, showing loyalty to restrictive measures and showing practical solutions to psychological problems with simple examples.

This book is intended for a wide range of readers; it can be useful for psychologists, students, teachers and public workers.

Enjoy your reading.

Social Isolation and Exit from Quarantine

Tatiana Semenova

Social Isolation and Exit from Quarantine

Olympia Publishers
London

www.olympiapublishers.com
OLYMPIA PAPERBACK EDITION

Copyright © Tatiana Semenova 2021

The right of Tatiana Semenova to be identified as author of this work has been asserted in accordance with sections 77 and 78 of the Copyright, Designs and Patents Act 1988.

All Rights Reserved

No reproduction, copy or transmission of this publication may be made without written permission.
No paragraph of this publication may be reproduced, copied or transmitted save with the written permission of the publisher, or in accordance with the provisions of the Copyright Act 1956 (as amended).

Any person who commits any unauthorised act in relation to this publication may be liable to criminal prosecution and civil claims for damage.

A CIP catalogue record for this title is available from the British Library.

ISBN: 978-1-80074-102-7

First Published in 2021

Olympia Publishers
Tallis House
2 Tallis Street
London
EC4Y 0AB

Printed in Great Britain

Disclaimer

Publisher's Note: The information in this book has been compiled by way of general guidance only. Nothing in this book is intended as an express or implied warranty of the suitability of any product or service. The reader wishing to use a product or service discussed in this book should first consult a specialist or professional to ensure suitability for the reader's particular lifestyle and environmental needs if necessary. Neither the author nor the publisher shall be liable or responsible for any loss or damage allegedly arising from any information or suggestion in this book. The opinions expressed in this book are the author's own and do not reflect the views of the publisher, author's employer, organization, committee or other group or individual.

Contents

Introduction 11

The consequences of isolation from a psychologist's point of view 13

Norm or pathology behavior 17

Psychiatry, basic disorders 24

Adult quarantine 29

Quarantine for children 42

The illusion of seeking the positive in isolation 59

Diagnostics of mental functions 63

Recommendations of exit from quarantine 70

Introduction

In 2020, in the science of psychology, the urgent topic of social isolation arose. The whole world at one point plunged into a global quarantine. We have witnessed how, one after another, countries of the world closed their borders and introduced severe restrictions on freedom of movement. These were forced measures to contain the pandemic of the new virus. In a short period of time, people who are in self-isolation have experienced many events, which subsequently affected and will be reflected in their psychological state. At the beginning of this whole path, society was divided into two categories, those who immediately realized the danger of the virus and those who negligently treated this information. The main reason was that humans have not had this experience in over a hundred years. Now many specialists want to help society adapt to new living conditions. The quarantine regime proved to be a daunting task for psychologists. Information received from available sources confirmed this and indicated the existence of problems. In psychology, there are many theoretical and practical works on human isolation, loneliness, quarantine, and the like. So, it is necessary to admit the fact that this is not enough, since the problems remain. Only by improving theoretical knowledge and introducing it into practice is it possible to solve all kinds of psychological problems.

At the initial stage, you should choose the most common problems that require a quick solution. The speed of response will also depend on the fact that a number of cases may collapse before progression begins.

Society should be timely informed about the issues that arise and interest it. Otherwise, the information will be distorted by society itself and psychologists will have to register and answer very strange questions.

The consequences of isolation from a psychologist's point of view

Any psychological experience, for example acquired in long-term isolation, has acute and delayed consequences. In one category of people, symptoms can proceed easily with little inner experiences, while in another category, on the contrary, isolation causes serious mental changes.

The main reason is that people adapt to a sudden situation at different rates. This is primarily due to the individual characteristics of the personality, temperament of people, the presence of concomitant diseases, psychological and social problems.

The term adaptation is basic in the evolution of all living things. At the beginning of the formation of mankind, the ability to adapt to the environment was the basis of survival. In modern times, before the appearance of this virus, people lived without global changes in their daily lives. Now people are faced with three problems: awareness, acceptance and implementation of the quarantine recommendations.

A very difficult psychological moment has formed— isolation is a new adaptation for the health and survival of all mankind.

Here it is necessary to indicate that each person is responsible for the spread of the virus and is a participant in the entire epidemiological process. When it appeared, the focus of attention shifted to the medical staff. They were the first to receive information with evidence of the contagiousness of the virus. Public opinion was ambivalent about the forced measures to save the lives of young people as a priority when choosing the patient's age. Many now cite statistics that indicate the correctness of this decision. The loss of human lives from the virus, injuries and suicides of employees who survived severe overloads and shocks are the tragic consequences of the pandemic.

From the first days, there was a strong belief that a cured person receives immunity and can no longer pose a threat to other people. However, there is evidence of cases of secondary infection. Also, the possibility of accidental or intentional infection of other people cannot be ruled out, for example, transmission of the virus through handshakes or tobacco smoke.

New foci of infection are constantly appearing in the world. Official health sources inform about the possibility of a second wave of the pandemic. It is believed that the new virus is 3.5 times more infectious than the influenza virus. If seasonal diseases are added to the new virus, this can lead to even more severe consequences.

Psychologists need to establish feedback between people explaining that each person is in the restrictions of freedom. In general, now it should be more alarming that many countries severely affected by the virus are in a hurry to get out of the self-isolation regime, using several stages—the phases of quarantine. The economies of such countries do not have the resources to be quarantined.

The economy is also a very fragile and important element of our lives. Some business units were able to earn big money in the strictest quarantine regime, which led to a misunderstanding of the rest of the people about the ethics of such actions. Especially when there were cases of overpricing of necessary goods.

Society is always worried about financial well-being. Therefore, countries are gradually lifting restrictive measures, despite the existing high percentage of asymptomatic carriers of the virus. These are people who do not even suspect that they are carriers. The ongoing diagnostics constantly reveal many such people.

There is a simple formula for success: the faster an individual can adapt to new conditions of life, the more likely he will be successful.

A contradiction appears. Evolutionary adaptation is a long process (millions of years). We had to adapt to social isolation in hours. At this pace, it is simply impossible to comfortably rebuild, both physically and psychologically.

Psychologists can help to quickly form the skills of adaptation to new conditions of life, in order to get through the consequences of social isolation more calmly and more easily.

In the course of numerous discussions about the possible ways of the appearance of the virus and the reasons for its transfer to humans, several theories have been put forward. The working version is the transition of the virus from animal to human through evolutionary transformation. Also, society has repeatedly raised the issue of artificially creating a virus in a secret laboratory and even attributed this topic to previously published works on the possible appearance of a pandemic in the future and the need to microchip people for total control of its spread.

Definitely, this information caused the purchase of bunkers and the departure of part of the population to the forest and to the sea!

The power of the virus is such that it takes life, directly affects and destroys the nervous system, intimidates and manipulates our will. Owing to its danger, people should follow the recommendations of official sources of information. It is necessary to respect the work and efforts of the people involved in measures to prevent and overcome the pandemic.

Norm or pathology behavior

For a long time, psychologists have been debating the concept of the norm and its boundaries. The most important and serious question is where the norm ends and pathology begins. It is impossible to unequivocally answer this question without using a number of related sciences, from philosophy to statistical data. For decades, doctors, psychologists, lawyers, and so on have developed criteria for the norms of behavior, receiving new data from the constantly changing world. Basically, each person in his own way tries to accept these norms. This is due to a simple unwillingness to follow imposed instructions, developed without the active participation of the individual and usually perceived as restrictive measures of something in the form of internal and / or external discontent (protests, riots). This behavior Dr Steven Taylor called psychological "reactance".

In a simple statement, we can say that people are used to seeing, in all undertakings aimed at society, the absence of their own interests.

Consequently, the work done by many specialists in the prevention and early exit from restrictive measures is not perceived properly by a significant part of the population of our planet.

It is very difficult to develop norms for all mankind, because each society or individual has an experience gained and / or acquired in the process of life, which is closely related to many factors: the country and its peculiarity, climatic conditions, the level of economic development and a host of other factors.

It is important to note that excessive coercion to educate or retrain life experience has a negative effect on the psyche of people, since the norms of behavior are laid down in early childhood and are difficult to correct in the future.

Well-designed personal incentives, interests for people, have a good effect on the solution of personal and general social programs.

The involvement of each person in a specific process is a fundamental condition for success for the entire society. It is necessary to constantly inform, show examples and involve people in the decision to leave the quarantine. This condition should in no way take away significant resources from people and devastate their budget. Only in this way will the individual begin to realize that his personality and the life of each person has value for all of us.

Nice conclusion to describe the ideal world model.

In fact, comprehension and implementation of recommendations in practice has a number of difficulties.

Depending on what kind of temperament a person belongs to, these features will affect the decision-making of his lifestyle, including in isolation.

In psychology, four types of temperament are distinguished (Hans Jürgen Eysenck).

The strongest temperament is Sanguine. An active person, with a quick reaction to all events, easily adapting to a changing situation. He is productive at work and is able to recover his spent energy in a short period of time.

Choleric is fast, but easily depleted owing to emotional instability. He has no balance of nervous processes, which sharply distinguishes him from a sanguine person. The choleric has a capacity for work, however, quickly gets tired and fizzles out.

Phlegmatic—on the contrary, he is slow and has a balanced mood background. In work, he is productive not because of speed, but because of perseverance and responsibility.

Melancholic—reacts sharply to external factors. He cannot restrain his feelings by an effort of will, he is impressionable, emotionally vulnerable. The most asthenic type of temperament.

I think choleric and melancholic people are inherently the most vulnerable in times of isolation and stress. But we must not forget that direct correspondences for these descriptions are rare in life. Most often we have mixed types of temperament. It all depends in what situations these qualities are manifested. The same person can be very productive and calm at one time period and completely unbearable and disinhibited under other circumstances.

I would also like to note one more feature in the character of people—this is the concept of extra- and introversion.

Extroverts. They are turned towards people. They have many friends and try to avoid being alone. They are characterized by sociability, a positive emotional attitude.

Relationships are difficult for introverts because, being insecure people, they experience anxiety in social relationships. They are turned inside their world, and rarely let strangers in there.

It is not hard to see that during the quarantine period, extroverts find themselves in a losing position. Deprived of the necessary communication and meetings, they experience longing and discomfort.

The situation is more serious if we consider not a mentally healthy person, but persons with mental instability and/or psychological pathology. Most often in psychology, the pathological development of the personality is in the borderline state between the norm and the pathology, for example: such personality traits as psychopathy.

Psychopathy is a strong accentuation of character. It is based on profound changes in personality and temperament.

Psychopathy has three types of differences from the

norm:

1) Social maladjustment of the personality, which leads to difficulties in fulfilling their social roles in the profession, family, society.

2) Totality—pronounced mental characteristics are manifested in all spheres of activity.

3) Stability and low reversibility are a given with which you will have to live your whole life. It is difficult to correct.

There are the following types of psychopathies (Peter Gannushkin, Karl Leonhard): excitable, inhibited (asthenic and psychasthenic), hysterical, paranoid, schizoid, unstable.

Psychopathy of the excitable type (epileptoids)—this type is characterized by emotional excitability, fits of anger, affects for any, even insignificant reason. Aggression is most often directed at offenders and loved ones, less often at oneself (in the form of self-harm, sometimes—attempts to commit suicide). These personalities have difficulties with communication, they are not kept at work, they are prone to the use of stimulating and illegal drugs.

Inhibited psychopathies are divided into asthenic and psychasthenic. Asthenic psychopathy is usually detected in childhood: fatigue, exhaustion, irritability, timidity, feelings of inferiority.

Those suffering from psychasthenic psychopathy are distinguished by indecision, anxiety, and suspiciousness. Owing to constant doubts, they are unable to make quick and correct decisions.

Psychopathies of the hysterical circle—the main

character trait of such patients is egocentrism, the desire to constantly be in the center of attention, demonstrative behavior, hysterical seizures, and pretense.

Paranoid psychopathy—the main feature is the formation of overvalued ideas (self-importance, jealousy, etc.). Patients are vindictive, suspicious, affectively tense, deprived of warmth, prone to conflicts.

Schizoid psychopathy—individuals of this type are distinguished by secrecy, isolation from reality, autism. They are characterized by emotional disharmony (a combination of increased sensitivity and emotional coldness), strangeness, and a tendency to philosophize.

Unstable psychopathies—the main criterion is lack of will, suggestibility, lack of internal attitudes. These people often use alcohol, drugs, join asocial company, and commit socially illegal actions.

People with pathological personality changes without any quarantine, experience great difficulties in everything, including adaptation.

For example, a schizoid without going outside, with a sharp change in regime and lifestyle, can plunge even more into his rich, but distorted world and completely break away from reality.

Epileptoid—will hate the whole world and, first of all, his environment, will torture everyone and everything, arranging household showdowns.

The hysteric will go into hysterics, the neurotic will get tics and insomnia, the emotionally labile will rush from depression to increased gaiety.

It may seem improbable that quarantine can lead the psyche into a state of insanity, but we must not forget how important for such people a measured, well-tested survival mechanism with its heavy accentuations of character is and how quickly they jump off these schemes with the slightest fluctuations in mood and external factors.

Let us dwell on the question of what factors provoke the transition from a normal state to a pathological unhealthy one.

This question is best answered by psychosomatics. Philosophers have been engaged in the interaction of soul and body since ancient times. The great Hippocrates, highlighting four types of temperament, drew attention to the fact that internal characteristics provoke the development of ailments. Sanguine people more often suffer from circulatory disorders, melancholic people experience stomach pains, and choleric and phlegmatic people have liver problems. This hypothesis was later described by Friedrich Nietzsche.

On the basis of the works of Goethe and Schiller, Sigismund Freud formulated the thesis—the unconscious guides consciousness.

In quarantine, a vivid psychosomatic relationship arises, provoking exacerbation of health problems. Chain of events: an unfavorable family and social situation, psycho-traumatic events form an individual's affective tension, experiences that gradually connect the neuroendocrine and autonomic systems that change the work of the whole organism.

Psychiatry, basic disorders

Psychologists primarily look for health in the individual, in contrast to such a science as psychiatry. Severe psychiatric disorders that go beyond psychopathy are the work of psychiatrists. Let's briefly consider the main disorders that can worsen during the period of social isolation:

Phobias

There are many fears. Usually, they are called in direct proportion to the essence of fear itself.

The term phobias are fears that cause disorders in an anxious-suspicious person. The most common phobias are fear of spiders and snakes, closed (claustrophobic) and open spaces, carcinophobia. We also list the fear of loneliness or vice versa of society, the fear of dirty hands, and with it the fear of contracting infectious diseases—which is relevant now.

Fear is a defensive reaction of the body of many animals to a physical or mental-psychic event in time (past, present, future).

It carries a deep meaning inherent in the survival instinct.

In humans, the fear of death and for some reason the snake is considered congenital and naturally is not a pathology. Consider a situation where fear becomes an obsession, paralyzing the will.

Virusophobia. It is based on the fear of contracting the virus and causing harm to one's health. It is normal and correct that we use prophylaxis, wash our hands, brush our teeth, rinse our mouth and use a mask during the seasonal flu epidemic, drink vitamins and strengthen our immunity. But in overly fastidious and often ill people, these rules develop into complex rituals brought to the point of absurdity, when hygiene degenerates into a neuropsychiatric disorder. Such individuals wash their hands at regular intervals for literally hours, they may even sleep in a mask, be afraid to go out and communicate with the whole world around them.

Of course, during a pandemic, this category of people has every reason to fear progress of this disease.

Panic

There are two types:
1) Situational, as a consequence of the stress of excessive exertion, the use of stimulating intoxicants and endocrine disorders. It is inherent in all people and most often occurs in emergency situations, to which we attribute a pandemic and its consequences.

Panic is a natural reaction of the human psyche and the whole body to stress, while stimulating substances are released into the blood, for example, adrenaline, stress hormones, which are the immediate cause of anxiety, fear, palpitations, feeling of lack of air, and more.

2) Panic personality disorder. Panic attacks suffered several times give rise to fear of recurrence of these conditions. People tend to avoid similar situations and, as a result, find themselves locked in four walls. The most difficult case is if the attacks first occur at home, then these people are afraid to stay at home alone, fearing repetitions of panic attacks.

Paranoia, delusional disorders

Paranoia is a false idea of a person about himself, at the heart of its delusional overvalued ideas. The most famous are megalomania (I am Napoleon), persecution mania (they want to poison me, rob me, and now also infect me).

Somatic disorder—hypochondria is your own distorted opinion about your health, looking for dangerous symptoms and diseases in yourself (I am terminally ill).

Pathological jealousy—"who did you talk to on the stairs for so long, huh?!"

Jealousy is a feeling of mistrust in the loyalty of a partner, the fear of losing him in a general or private state (in which you knew and accepted him earlier), unwillingness to share him with others.

It develops especially sharply with great emotional, material and other types of attachment.

Let's look at a few examples that will help show how

different and dangerous jealousy can be.

The first situation is when two participants in a relationship are equally successful and hardworking, strive to be social and want to see positive progress in the relationship. However, both of them or one of them may develop distrust. It may or may not be justified. For psychologists, this situation is not alarming; it usually goes away on its own and does not have serious consequences.

Pathological jealousy is an obsessive condition that progresses and poses a real danger to people.

As a rule, such subjects have a certain sense of inferiority, that there are people much better than them. They live in fear that at the first opportunity their love object will go to another. Experiencing excruciating torment, some live in the constant provision of evidence of their superiority, trying to emphasize their best qualities and presenting their half with all kinds of gifts. Other jealous people plunge into a manic state of psychosis when jealousy becomes the main emotion in a relationship—destroying it. Pathological jealousy (Othello's syndrome) is the main cause of domestic quarrels that end in domestic violence and other tragic consequences.

The main task of psychologists when working with morbid jealousy is to identify such cases early, using well-proven methods and working together with psychiatrists and social protection organizations.

Delusional disorders

Delusional disorders are severe psychiatric disorders, most often associated with schizophrenia and progressing over time. Allocate hallucinatory delirium—visual, auditory and mental hallucinations.

Depression

One of the most common mental disorders. The main symptoms are: a lowered background of mood, up to a complete absence of emotions (stupor), apathy—unwillingness and inability to take any action (until complete immobilization). It can be noted that depression is also possible in mentally healthy people. In pathology, it is part of a manic-depressive psychosis, when depression is replaced by the opposite stage of mania, in which a person has an increased mood background—laughs, sings, dances, speaks loudly, gesticulates, and the like, forgetting about sleep and being in a state of euphoria for several days.

Adult quarantine

Different age groups experience social isolation in different ways.

For young, successful careerists who spend most of their time at work outside the home, this confinement can be extremely stressful. This category of people experiences many unpleasant emotions associated with missed earning opportunities and professional growth. An unfinished quasi-need arises, especially when an important project at work is suddenly interrupted.

Quasi-need (Kurt Lewin) is a state of tension that occurs in the process of achieving a goal. It is an intermediate element between the emergence of a true need and its satisfaction. Quasi-need can temporarily pass into a latent state: it is not actually experienced by a person, but nevertheless does not lose its significance, and in the subconscious, it forms a conflict of an unfinished action, which causes anxiety, discomfort and stress in the subject.

Stress is a set of psychophysical processes that arise in a sudden situation, which the body perceives as hostile.

Under favorable conditions, acute stress passes, and under unfavorable conditions, it turns into a state of neuropsychic stress (distress), which forms various pathological personality changes.

Of course, stress resistance is associated with the type of personality, individual characteristics of a person's reaction to a situation, and the level of self-control of behavior.

In quarantine, we first of all experience information stress; it arises in a situation of an information boom, when describing catastrophes and tragedies, when a pile of negative messages is thrown onto the subject, which do not fit into the worked-out perception scheme and form an emotional reaction of anxiety, danger. Note that, in addition to emotions, physiological mechanisms are involved in the process of stress development—nervous disorders, cardiac pathologies, and more.

Stress lowers resistance to diseases, including infectious diseases (adaptation disease, Hans Selye).

The next group of young people is married couples with children, for whom social isolation becomes a positive factor in strengthening the family—more free time appears to be devoted to children. Such parents are usually creative individuals themselves and can independently teach and engage their children in pre-prepared lessons.

Diversity in parenting approaches is often associated with family financial well-being.

Wealthy families experience discomfort from social

isolation, since their rhythm of life does not coincide with restrictive measures. They use every opportunity to bring in many individual professionals to develop their children. These include private lessons with a tutor at home or in educational, creative and sports centers. For a number of features, the parents of this group are often unable to organize children's leisure time themselves.

On the one hand, adult single people should have more opportunities and therefore less worry about the established quarantine, since they do not have family obligations; nevertheless, they feel discomfort in their own way. As a result of isolation, they may experience increased feelings of loneliness and forgetfulness, especially in older people.

The lack of personal meetings and walks in the fresh air introduces them into a depressing state, which can provoke an exacerbation of chronic diseases.

Exacerbation of chronic conditions

When information appeared about the new virus, its danger and lack of knowledge, people felt stress on themselves. This mental state provokes an exacerbation of physical ailments and is confirmed by data from psychosomatics (the science of the interaction of the mental and physical state of people).

Naturally, the most serious diseases are cardiovascular pathology and oncology. Diseases of the nervous system, nervous breakdowns and stress provoke their exacerbation in quarantine. Owing to the fact that medical institutions are overcrowded with infectious patients, people with chronic diseases find themselves in a specific position. They had to postpone visits to doctors for a long time, which negatively affected their health.

Planned operations were postponed; even a simple visit to the dentist became unavailable, except in emergency cases.

Family relationships

Family relationships are a closed and poorly studied topic. As the saying goes, "all families are equally happy and unhappy in their own way."

Family psychology distinguishes different types of adult relationships. There are traditional and non-traditional alliances, legal and free relationships. The reality today is that young people have no interest or opportunity to start families. They see and react faster and more sensitively to all changes in the world. Some, in search of stability and well-being, choose to create a family or union with a large age difference. Developed countries are registering an increase in inter-ethnic marriages. Thanks to the constantly implemented state support for large families, such families have been preserved. Of course, in developing and even developed countries, the problem of supporting large families is very urgent.

Now let's take a look at a few cornerstones in family relationships during quarantine. The family was closed on their territory. Whether it is a large territory or a small apartment is of great importance, since every person, including a child, has the right to personal space. Even if the whole family has the same desires or needs, this does not mean that everyone will be happy from it. For example, children want to play and make noise, parents also do not mind keeping their children in a good mood, but at a moderate pace.

Housing repairs were suspended during quarantine— many neighbors could not stand the annoying noise.

Spacious housing is beneficial for families also because of the established social distance—at least two meters between people, as the main prevention against infection. Since the majority of residents live in apartment buildings, this recommendation is very difficult. A simple example with adjoining balconies between neighbors (smoking on the balconies), using the elevator, stairs and so on.

The absence of the usual rhythm of life for everyone in the family caused the discovery of many hidden states and even secrets, married couples were not happy to find out.

Small housing is a test for any, even the most harmonious relationship. In this case, tightness is not closeness, it is punishment. How easy it was earlier to resolve the brewing conflict simply by going out into the street. This is an everyday psychology, but it has a well-developed scheme—to take time out, cool down, rethink, speak out to someone else about your problems and come home with a different mood, ready for dialogue and compromise. Quarantine cut off this important opportunity to leave the heated debate for a short time.

By the way, in such cases it is not advisable to seek salvation from "ringing in the ears", hanging around on the street (especially in the dark); believe me, there are much better solutions.

Naturally, isolation itself is not the root cause of family problems; such unions have previously lived in difficult relationships. If the family often raises questions that are difficult to answer or fulfill orders, make it a rule not to solve them right away. Nevertheless, do not show your selfishness—create favorable conditions for the life of the family, even if a divorce is brewing ahead. In the event of a divorce, you will need health and money more than ever.

As any lawyer will say, it is important that the service has a time frame and an accurate cost. Then people easily perceive such information.

Likewise, in a family it is important not to scatter in corners and ask someone else's opinion all the time, but to take and solve dead-end situations in harmony, love and mutual respect. Mature individuals find the resources to resolve differences in a civilized way.

Please do not arrange "family performances" on the

streets of your beloved city!

Loss of job or income

Many of us value stability. But even the best business projects don't last forever. Business, like the rest of the world, needs to react quickly and adapt to new realities. Fortunately, there are people who are ready to help. They say that there is work everywhere and there is a lot of it. But the point is different; you need to answer the question of whether a person who has lost his job is ready to instantly reorganize and go to a new one, especially if it is extremely responsible. People who have lost their jobs often have a feeling of injustice, failure, providence of fate (for those who believe in it). In some countries, the society condemns unemployed people—making it clear that idleness is bad first of all for itself. Knowledgeable people would refrain from such comments, realizing that anyone can get into such a situation. Losing a job is a trial and additional psychological distress. A person should be able to be useful, to be part of society and deservedly receive a reward for his contribution, both in monetary terms and non-material. All over the world, the topic of increasing labor freedoms for workers and job seekers is relevant.

Here's a classic example: some farmers in Italy had to harvest. Agricultural workers from another country responded to their aid.

It can be difficult for psychologists to prepare general

guidelines for people who have lost their jobs. All cases must be considered strictly individually. There are situations when emotions outweigh the logic of behavior; a person who has lost a job, instead of looking for another job, goes into depression, begins to consume alcohol, which in turn does not help, but makes the situation even more difficult. In this case, one can only hope that the family, relatives or neighbors, knowing about his harmful weaknesses, will be able to coordinate efforts in time to prevent the plunge into depression.

Acquired addictions during isolation

The topic of addictions was and will be relevant in all countries of the world. Today, you can legally or very simply buy alcohol, tobacco, energy drinks, synthetic stimulants, and so on. More and more countries are legalizing and expanding the list of addictive drugs. Only recently has the spread of e-cigarettes, which harmed teenagers the most, been reversed, succumbing to new trends and aggressive advertising.

There are super-rich people who, by their behavior in society and the media, not only freely talk about the legalization of drugs, but also use them on the air. Which is extremely unacceptable.

Everyone knows the consequences of using the above drugs—severe addiction, withdrawal symptoms (the so-called withdrawal symptoms), poisoning, overdose, oncology, gastritis, infectious diseases, hallucinations (delirium tremens), and further complete personality degradation and dementia. Through addictions, including addiction to gambling, sectarianism—people lose their families, material wealth, property. They also remain unemployed, end up in psychiatric clinics and correctional institutions. Nevertheless, the trend of an increase in addictive people is growing every year on a massive scale. Since the beginning of this year, there has been a sharp jump in alcohol sales. Demand has arisen from the ability to give up driving, rumors that alcohol protects against the virus and fears of a shortage of this "irreplaceable" product in stores.

The final straw was that people attending Alcoholics Anonymous were deprived of this opportunity to fight their addiction.

The second most serious addiction in quarantine is a non-standardized computer pastime. People went online. Long-term use of electronic devices is fraught with consequences—possible radiation exposure, impaired vision, posture, headaches, and insomnia. In the virtual world, there is a dulling of reality, the substitution of concepts and a decrease in interest in real life.

Each day in the quarantine began with a new roundup of news about the number of deaths, new infections, complications and recovered. This negative information naturally provokes a high level of anxiety in people, which in turn aggravates addictions to computers, alcohol, as a way to relieve stress and escape from the harsh reality into a world of dreams.

News resources for impressionable people began to set special filters for negative news.

Some of society, on the contrary, became dependent on negative news; they are distinguished by a lack of empathy (compassion) for world problems.

Social networks, communication, creativity and income

The self-isolation regime forced people to use the Internet more intensively. In the digital world, all basic user functions have been around for at least 15 years. Multimedia content, video calls, downloading, transferring and publishing large amounts of data, forced Internet service providers to limit the speed on network devices. Many employers, schools and universities quickly and easily were able to adapt to remote work. Of course, from time to time there were slight difficulties with organizing control and checking the progress of schoolchildren and students, but in general the digital world was well prepared for new conditions.

In the process of immersion in strict quarantine, people began to feel a sense of distrust in various information.

While some dreamed of restoring their old life, others looked for the negative from the self-isolation regime in every news. For example, there were attempts to destroy 5G cell towers; the reason for this was the posted information about the dangers of these technologies and their connection with the incidence of the coronavirus.

When covering the issues of politics and political literacy of the population, an understanding arose about the need to introduce a balance between censorship and publicity. Social networks, owing to the awareness of their responsibility and receiving a lot of complaints, have come to a state in which the size, inconsistency, and suppression of information began to generate aimless discussions and initiated checks. In the future, it will be interesting to see the work of political news moderators.

In a number of recent events in the digital world, attention should be paid to an attempt to establish total control over the movement of each person through the introduction of software tools on smartphones in order to prevent the spread of the pandemic. This was seen as a violation of privacy rights. Operating system manufacturers have created an API wrapper for transferring user data to future tracking programs—mobile applications. In this case, it is assumed that the user will install the application on his smartphone and will share personal and geographic data with the administrators of the systems—programs.

By agreeing to the installation of such applications, you can become a participant in an accidental software failure, erroneous enrollment in the quarantine list, or be harassed.

Since about 2005, people have actively immersed themselves in work and creativity using social platforms on the Internet. Many people find this, a convenient means for communication, self-realization, a way to declare themselves, to talk about their achievements in interesting projects. However, the other side of the digital world is also known. Every Internet user should be aware of the important rule that downloadable content is more likely to remain there forever and can be copied and / or changed many times not in your favor and published without your permission.

Social networks are extremely slow to respond to requests to remove inappropriate content. For example, in one well-known network, there are only a few templates by which people can select a situational question and send it to the support service. Unfortunately, standard requests for existing problems are not enough, and even those that exist in the system are a monologue of users. The inability to have a timely, simple and free, fully fledged dialogue between representatives of social networks and their clients (without involving lawyers) is very annoying and puts the latter in unequal rights.

The goal of a psychologist is to prepare people for possible risks from their own actions and those of a third party. If you add failures from communication on social networks to the self-isolation regime, then a strong negative background will form, which will affect a person for a long time, owing to the publicity and availability of published data.

Social media news tends to be extreme. This is due to the specifics of the networks themselves—they were developed according to the algorithm: put a like and this is "true"—since most cannot be mistaken in their choice. This algorithm is extremely dangerous for many reasons. For example, the richest and / or most famous people will always have unequal opportunities for success in such networks. Let's clarify: to create high quality art photography requires a lot of money. It is highly doubtful that low-quality and cheap multimedia content can please you and your future fans. Social networks are primarily advertising and communication with a bright emotional accent. Probably many people open personal and work pages and want to get some benefit from them. There is a strong belief that social media can make good money. Unfortunately, this is not true. Most of them do not make direct payments to your account and for your activity. Usually, people make money on advertising from lucrative contracts, and social networks remain just a tool to increase its circulation.

So the dream of many people has come true to go into the digital world and return only when they call for dinner!

Our recommendations for the use of social networks are based on the creation and maintenance of Internet pages without prejudice to your health. You have to understand that this is real work. The main thing is to find a balance of your physical and psychological forces between capabilities, desire, necessity and routine.

Quarantine for children

Before the introduction of quarantine measures, children went to school, walked in the fresh air and the next day they were at home, with similar conditions of restrictions as in adults.

Psychologists divide childhood into several groups, and each of them will react differently to isolation.

Infants and young age. Doctors recommend that parents with newborns take three walks on the street. This improves the state of the nervous system, is the main prevention of rickets (moderate sunbathing contributes to the production of vitamin D). Isolation can negatively affect the development of newborns, increasing anxiety, irritability. Some children have a decrease in appetite and immunity.

Families with babies find themselves in a difficult situation; caring for a baby requires constant purchases of baby food, hygiene products, routine checkups from a pediatrician, and the like. In quarantine, all this became very problematic.

Everyone knows that a child in a moving wheelchair calms down, faster.

However, walks on the balcony only partially replaced

the fully fledged walking on the street. The legislation of many countries does not protect non-smokers from the smoke of their neighbors who smoke. Therefore, many people were deprived of the only opportunity to access fresh air.

For young children, the leading activity is the development of speech and walking. In quarantine, they experienced a shortage of live communication with relatives and other children. Parents are strongly encouraged to talk to them more often, to use books and techniques to promote speech development. For physical development, it is necessary to use exercises aimed at general muscle groups, coordination of movements.

Preschoolers. This is an interesting and important period in the formation of the psyche. Thinking and cognitive processes begin to develop rapidly. The experience of imagining fantasies appears, which is acquired through play.

Parents should develop in children memory and attention, fine motor skills of hands (preparation for writing), stimulate volitional behavior (self-control). These listed, higher mental functions are the main indicators of a child's readiness for school.

Usually, preparation for school takes place in kindergartens and developmental childcare centers outside the home.

Parents now have organizational tasks:
1) Ensure the development of their children independently, based on their experience and available

literature with teaching aids.

2) Arrange childcare if both parents continue to work outside the home during quarantine and kindergartens are closed.

School age. The leading activity of this age is study. During quarantine, several groups of schoolchildren experienced difficulties. First graders came to school for the first time and studied for only half of the school year, not having time to fully adapt to the new environment. The junior and senior classes faced the problem of certification, the transition to another educational level. A high-quality educational process should be continuous and full time for schoolchildren and students. In quarantine mode, I had to switch to distance learning, which has a number of features discussed in the next paragraph.

Online education

The transition from full-time education to distance learning was relatively smooth for students. But schools and teachers experienced tense times, as they had to master training programs in a short time and structure lessons in new ways. Many teachers report that they have increased their workload, burnout and fatigue by switching to distance learning. All this is due to the large amount of digital information that had to be processed for each student.

The children, in turn, reacted differently to the change in the form of education.

Some very quickly and with interest plunged into the online, others experienced the difficulties of such lessons and assignments. Such education is not new, and many countries with hard-to-reach and sparsely populated areas have extensive distance learning experience.

Another category that often uses the online process is children with disabilities or gifted children who choose international schools as their basic or additional education.

Let's list the main positive and negative aspects of distance education.

Pros:

1) By far the most important plus is a flexible schedule, the ability to view lessons at any time and in any place where there is Internet. The morning rush, problems with transport, traffic jams, weather conditions disappear. A slight malaise will not be a reason for falling behind in the program. Such learning opens up more freedom, without the orders and supervision of teachers and the interpersonal relationships of classmates.

2) Geographic independence. Students can choose high-quality and specialized education in any country of the world in any language, taking into account their individual interests and abilities, while staying at home. It became possible to replace one course with another or the entire school, if necessary.

3) Tuition fees—as a rule, it is lower and parents do not have to spend their budget on school uniforms, meals, transport. When choosing an international school, the savings are significant (there are no costs for placing a

child abroad, including visa, insurance, accommodation, meals, flights and payment of a guardian, tutor).

4) Accessibility to different groups of students—as noted earlier, everyone, even children with disabilities or those who for many reasons cannot find their place in the peer group, have the opportunity to receive education at home.

5) Communication relationship with teachers. Owing to their personal characteristics, many students find it more comfortable to find information on the Internet themselves than to show their incompetence and directly ask for help from the teacher.

Talented and hardworking independent students make progress in their studies.

6) Amount of information. No textbook or teacher compares to the wealth of knowledge the web provides. The child himself chooses in what form and style to receive this information—read, listen, watch videos, multimedia and all this with good graphics is colorful and interesting.

7) Security. It should be conditionally divided into physical, psychological and informational. Children are at home, which means they have fewer safety concerns. The likelihood of street incidents, road traffic accidents, of negative cases on the school grounds, and the like is reduced.

Online education excludes direct contacts between people and improves the epidemiological situation in the world.

Obviously, physical security is a plus when choosing online training.

From a psychological point of view, it is impossible to say unequivocally that such training will have a beneficial effect on the development of the psyche. First of all, the skills of social communication and interaction in a team can suffer—we will consider these aspects a little below, including information security.

Minuses:

1) In the first place, of course, there is no Internet or poor connection. Today in the world, 30 percent of students do not have the opportunity to use online lessons.

2) Organization of the workplace. For remote education, it is required to provide a fully-fledged workplace, a desk, a computer and a separate room for each student. It is necessary to provide a working atmosphere and quietness. For large families, this can be an urgent problem.

3) Small children do not have independent skills to master complex computer technologies. This is the main category of children for whom online education is not suitable in principle. They cannot sit for the whole lesson at the computer without being distracted and listening to a teacher who is not there. Their learning is directly related to practice and play, and online time should be strictly limited according to their age. Many doctors generally do not recommend teaching a child to a computer before he turns six years old.

4) For many working parents, school is not only an educational tool, but also a "second home" where their children spend all their time under the supervision of teachers while they are at work. Distance education is possible only if adults are present at home.

5) Weak control. It becomes more difficult for teachers to test the true knowledge of students without face-to-face visual control, and students are naturally more tempted to use cheating assistive devices. It also increases the responsibility of parents, who must constantly check the presence of the child in online lessons, and not online, in games or contacts.

6) The individual abilities of the student. This form of teaching is not suitable for all children, since it implies responsibility, efficiency at the computer, self-control, and most importantly the ability to independently structure your work, hand over completed assignments on time and conscientiously attend all lessons, carefully listening to the teacher's instructions. In our time, it is far from easy to teach infantile weak-willed children to work independently and to motivate them.

7) Lack of direct contact. Remote lessons are devoid of live communication, spontaneity, and improvisation. It takes a very creative teacher to get students interested using only the monitor screen.

8) Lack of practice. If the network copes with theoretical data even better than ordinary lessons, then of course, in the practical part, the online fails—a complete fiasco, from laboratory classes in chemistry and physics to physical education, music …

9) There are risks of choosing low-quality training

courses, programs and even entire educational institutions without educational licenses and accreditations, which have very colorful advertising and paint bright prospects, but in fact they just make money on schoolchildren, students and their parents without providing appropriate services approved by the Ministry of Education.

It is recommended to carefully study the contracts for the training of students in order to obtain a quality education.

The conclusion on the advantages and disadvantages of online education described above can be formulated as follows:

Students should continually work on their weaknesses, using and developing their abilities where they have achieved good results, and parents or guardians should make efforts to provide students with everything necessary for overall success.

Computer addiction

More than once in this book the question of computer addiction has been touched upon, but now we want to dwell on this problem directly in children. How often parents demand to turn off the computer or TV and switch to another activity, and unfortunately, they see that every day it becomes more difficult for the child to do, as he feels an increasing need for electronic devices to the detriment of the rest.

There are several signs of the formation of computer addiction:

1) Time frame. Parents notice that the younger generation spends a lot of time at the computer, losing their sense of proportion. Abrupt mood swings, superficial communication with parents, negativity and emptiness, fits of anger—all these are the consequences of being too much at the computer.

Users always have prepared arguments in advance, justifications for their constant activity, accompanied by irritability.

2) Decreased interests and lack of friends outside the network. The quality of modern computers, devices and digital content is quickly addictive. Fueled by the monetary success of some bloggers and the worldwide trend of bragging, it also contributes negatively to the formation of a normal psyche. Children choose a preference for multiplayer computer games, create or fall into groups of more experienced gamers who require high success rates and are able to manipulate newcomers.

Social networks and more highly specialized digital platforms, such as Instagram, YouTube, often contain inappropriate content for young people, provoking them to take risks and imposing their interests.

Please note that the age for opening accounts on digital platforms must be over 13 years old.

There is a threat of imitation of false idols. Some actions from popular people also raise many questions.

The cult of personality reduces the development of individuality and forms imitative behavior.

3) Health. Computer addiction negatively affects many systems and human organs.

Vision—red eye syndrome and decreased visual acuity, double vision, strabismus and astigmatism. It is especially dangerous to use devices with bright screens in the dark.

Poor posture—scoliosis, deformity of the hand, carpal tunnel syndrome.

Intestinal problems—constipation and hemorrhoids from prolonged sitting position and physical inactivity, immobilization in general.

Neurological problems—tics, headaches, malnutrition and sleep disorders, neuralgia and neuroses.

Psychological and social changes—limitation of interests—fixation on one game, conversations only on the topic of computer technology. Decreased academic performance, lack of other motivation.

All these symptoms appear and increase gradually. In strong and healthy children, they will be insignificant, while children with poor health may develop serious mental and physical problems.

In practice, many more signs may emerge that indicate changes in the health and behavior of young people, but it is not only computer addiction that causes them.

It's easy to get used to a computer, but hard to wean. It all starts with a simple situation—children see a beautiful device, smartphone, computer, new digital device in the hands of their parents, friends, and want to get the same by copying their behavior. Modern life, advertising, makes you immerse yourself in these technologies from childhood. Parents often take pride in and praise their children for learning new things.

At the beginning, adults do not notice the problems that their child devotes a lot of time to computer technologies—it is rather beneficial for them that he stays at home and does not distract the older generation from business or leisure. Over time, the emergence of addiction to a digital device becomes obvious, and any ban on it provokes aggression, literally turns into a "war" for pressing the switch off button.

Psychologists note that if a child has developed a computer addiction that has become the meaning of life, and without it he can no longer calmly spend the day, then such a problem cannot be solved overnight in any way—simply by taking away the device. An abrupt change of scenery can end in running away from home, injuring himself or those who have deprived him of his "toy", as well as tantrums and general psychosis.

Severe addiction requires a step-by-step solution with the help of specialists. You shouldn't think that this is a trifling problem. For example, in Finland, a young man with this ailment is not taken into the army, as he is considered an unsuitable and dangerous subject. By the way, this country is one of the first to practice online technologies in education for a long time, because its weather conditions and territorial remoteness do not allow many students to attend schools and they study remotely.

There was a negative connection between the

opportunity to get an education without leaving home and the emergence of addiction.

The same thing now happens during isolation. Parents had to put their children at computers for educational needs, but in addition to this, they got even more immersed in the network, and the children with whom work was carried out to reduce the time at the computer were again inseparable from their "friend and foe" at the same time.

If earlier school, homework and extra classes occupied most of their time, now all their activities are concentrated in the network and aggravated the pathological state of attachment to gadgets.

Of course, not only quarantine is to blame for this problem.

Parents and guardians should organize work to prevent computer addiction. It is necessary to have a short discussion every day about the dangers and benefits of computer technology. Show professional thematic examples and explain that the child's body is not able to withstand the rhythm of an adult user's activity.

It is definitely a long process of integrating a healthy attitude towards modern innovation.

With well-formed work at the device, an agreed time limit, good rest in between and after classes, the ability to captivate students with a variety of hobbies that are not directly related to a computer, and most importantly, the ability to build warm trusting relationships with their children—all this can help smooth out the situation in which the child got and correct the differences that have arisen.

Physical inactivity

Physical inactivity is a decrease in physical activity and, in connection with this, a weakening of muscle tone. This phenomenon is directly caused by a sedentary lifestyle.

One of the main reasons is an increase in educational standards owing to which students are forced to spend a long time at school at their desks and at home doing their homework. An important factor in the formation of hypodynamia is the material wealth of the family, since all sports sections where the child could strengthen his muscles are paid and inaccessible, including geographically.

There are not enough sports grounds on the street, and if earlier children could visit school stadiums for sports, now all schools have a closed area that cannot be reached outside classes.

Also, recently, in many parts of the world, weather conditions make it difficult to do sports on the street.

A serious factor in the decrease in physical activity in children is the lack of interest in sports activities. Modern teenagers prefer to spend their free time sitting in front of the TV and computer, instead of playing on the street and other physical activity. They do not have basic skills to do simple exercises and warm-ups.

Quarantine also contributed to the development of physical inactivity.

Let us briefly list the consequences of prolonged decrease in physical activity. First of all, this is lethargy and weakness, impaired muscle tone, loss of endurance and performance. This is followed by a violation of blood supply and outflow of lymph, a decrease in heart rate and respiration. A separate hot topic is excess weight, obesity, diabetes.

Physical inactivity is a consequence of computer addiction. Together, they provoke poor posture, eye diseases, varicose veins, constipation and hemorrhoids, nervous diseases and other ailments.

These symptoms develop gradually in both children and adults. It is pertinent to recall the statement:

Movement is life.

We will form a few simple tips for the prevention of physical inactivity and its above-mentioned consequences in quarantine.

You need to organize your workplace according to all the rules of ergonomics (with good lighting, an adjustable office chair and table). The distance from the monitor screen should be equal to your arm's length. If the child's feet do not reach the floor, a support is needed. Believe me, this is really very important.

Every hour, and for small children half an hour, you need to take a break and warm up, change your posture, move away from the table, and look into the distance.

During the quarantine, home fitness classes became

relevant. Yoga, Pilates, aerobics and dancing can give you and your children new experiences, improve health, and you can feel creativity even in such cramped conditions.

Search for hobbies and entertainment

At all times, the topic of children's leisure is subject to discussion. The rapid development of civilization every year brings more and more opportunities for the formation of new types of hobbies and entertainment for children.

Of course, digital technologies are in the lead ahead of the "planet of all". They have become especially in demand in quarantine.

Online study and communication with relatives, friends, search for new interests, books, games, videos on YouTube—everything or almost everything can be found online for a child. We have listed that computer technology is fraught with an invisible danger—addiction and all the ensuing consequences. Therefore, the task of parents and guardians, teachers and psychologists are to use the Internet correctly, respecting the restrictions. It is necessary to explain to children that the main task of the network is to obtain information for further development, which should have a positive effect on the child's psyche. And the main limitation is not to visit unverified or prohibited sites and have a set time limit for digital devices.

To reduce fatigue, take frequent breaks and shift children's attention to dynamic physical activities. As part of everyday circumstances, you can combine everyday activities with health benefits, for example, teach them to collect scattered toys.

The hobby should be related to the age of the child. Each period of development has its own leading activity (Lev Vygotsky), which must be developed:

At an early age, this is personal communication with parents, the development of motor skills and speech.

At preschool age, all mental functions should be developed through play, and at school age through study.

In high school, communication with peers and the search for a profession becomes a priority.

It should not be forgotten that sometimes desire does not coincide with capabilities and abilities.

Children often live with illusions and fantasies, not imagining the real side of their hobby. It is necessary to delicately and smoothly guide and prompt the child the right way to choose, more often use examples from life, so as not to destroy the childhood dream, to get positive emotions and health improvement from the chosen hobby, and not vice versa.

The question is especially relevant for adolescents when choosing a further profession. There are a lot of factors that have to be taken into account in this crucial period. This includes academic performance in specialized subjects, physical data, the number of places in the university, tuition fees, territorial location, and so on. Desire is definitely not enough—there is reality and it dictates its own rules.

In conclusion, I would like to add that no matter what entertainment the child chooses, find an opportunity to be interested in his free pastime, encourage creativity and development, be his friend and ally and guide him in the direction where he could succeed in the future.

The illusion of seeking the positive in isolation

With the introduction of the self-isolation regime, life has changed a lot. Restrictions have forced all of us to look for ways to adapt to quarantine and the optimal way out of it.

With each experience, people shared their disturbing thoughts and offered different ideas. Thus, a general confused consciousness was formed. Not all thoughts were rational owing to the influence of stress.

It is important for psychologists to convey to society the correct mechanism for responding to quarantine, based on common sense and a positive attitude. A well-known comparative analysis can help with this.

Consider in parallel the positive and negative aspects of the consequences of quarantine:

1) Allergists note a decrease in seasonal exacerbations of allergic rhinitis, bronchitis and asthma, due to the fact that everyone wears masks and appears less on the street. The level of contact with the allergen is reduced and symptoms are mildly tolerated. Not everyone can wear masks with contraindications. Before quarantine, allergy sufferers did not comply with the recommendation to use respirators, fearing to look unusual on the street. Constant wearing of a mask in the

long term can negatively affect human health.

2) Family reunion. A long stay at home helps to strengthen family relationships. In less harmonious families and families that have been separated through circumstances, a number of serious disagreements can arise.

3) Mastering online technologies. The younger generation uses the network every day to achieve goals, to the detriment of their health (computer addiction, physical inactivity). In people over 40, owing to physiological characteristics, computers cause irritation, fatigue and a desire to abandon them. A significant part of the population does not have access to these technologies at all.

4) Introverts and just very shy, uncommunicative people benefit from reducing direct social contact, using it as a prevention of the spread of infection. Long-term lack of live communication in both introverts and extroverts can provoke depression.

5) Free time—home projects (home improvement, minor repairs, cleaning), education (language courses, reading) and other things. Projects are usually solved quickly, unlike education; however, the daily routine leaves a period of time that is difficult to fill with various tasks in self-isolation mode. The monotony of the rhythm causes a desire for changes in life.

6) Environmental shift. There was a consumer slump during the quarantine. Factories have reduced the production of unclaimed goods. The load on waste incineration and oil refineries and transport has decreased, which, in general, has led to a reduction in

emissions of harmful substances into the earth's atmosphere. After the removal of restrictive measures, environmental indicators returned to the same level, plus the burden of collection and disposal of used synthetic masks and other medical supplies was added.

7) The most positive effect of quarantine is the quarantine itself. These measures helped to reduce the spread of infection and unloaded the work of medical services. There was additional time for doctors and scientists to develop treatment methods, purchase the necessary equipment, search for effective prevention and vaccination. As a result, the number of cured patients began to increase, and mortality began to decline, but we should not lose our vigilance, since the virus continues to pose a danger. The consumer recession caused by the quarantine led to multimillion-dollar job cuts (increased unemployment and social inequality).

8) Isolation has brought people together around the world. There was a social solidarity for all people involved in the quarantine exit process. The main goal is to preserve the health and life of people; the next goal is to solve social and economic problems to maintain society. Therefore, it is important for psychologists to explain to society that the events that are taking place have a logically constructed model of getting out of quarantine for all countries of the world, and under any circumstances people should show the best human traits of character, in order to avoid riots and chaos in society.

This chapter has examined some of the positive and negative patterns that can cause controversy about the breadth and depth of the required detail.

The experience of people is mostly negative and carries physical, psychological suffering and pain. It is difficult to explain phrases about quarantine as a positive moment in people's lives. Most likely there is a desire of people to distract themselves from negative news and try to find positive aspects in restrictive measures. This behavior comes from physiology—the body's protective function is turned on, which should regulate the amount of negative information within the framework of the general psychological state of a person.

The uniqueness of the situation lies in its scale and the speed of involving people from different social groups in a single global problem.

Diagnostics of mental functions

Taking into account the circumstances of isolation, we offer you options for diagnosing the mental parameters of children and adults, which may be relevant for study in quarantine. We tried to choose methods suitable for self-realization and aimed primarily at knowing oneself. **Not to diagnose (this is a doctor's job), but to study and learn something new about yourself and your family.**

Tests should have: relative ease of use, speed of implementation, complementarity and demonstration of changes in the observed signs.

Personality tests used to study psychosomatic characteristics, which are essential for social adaptation and regulation of behavior:

- The Sixteen Personality Factor Questionnaire (16PF)—Raymond Cattell, also (14PF) for adolescents 12-18 years old; and (12PF) for children 8-12 years old.
- The Minnesota Multiphasic Personality Inventory (MMPI)

The questionnaires of Hans Eysenck will help to find out the level of neuroticism / stability, psychoticism / socialisation and indicator of extraversion / introversion:

- The Eysenck Personality Inventory (EPI)

- The Eysenck Personality Questionnaire (EPQ)
- The Eysenck Personality Profiler (EPP)

Determine the type of temperament allows method of David Keirsey:
- The Keirsey Temperament Sorter (KTS)

To study the level of anxiety as a property of the psyche and state of a person, can be applied following diagnostics by Charles Spielberger:
- The State-Trait Anxiety Inventory for adults (STAI-AD), (STAI-CH) for children
- The State-Trait Personality Inventory (STPI)—designed for adults, where present extra scale, anger, curiosity, depression.

In this group, we also recommend:
- The Taylor Manifest Anxiety Scale (TMAS)—Janet Taylor
- The Zung Self-Rating Anxiety Scale (SAS)—William W.K. Zung

To identify the severity of the depressive state will help:
- The Hamilton Rating Scale for Depression (HRSD)—Max Hamilton
- The Zung Self-Rating Depression Scale (SDS)—William W.K. Zung

Actual method of diagnosing the level of subjective feeling of loneliness, was developed at the University of California, Los Angeles:

- The UCLA Loneliness Scale (UCLA)—M.L. Ferguson, Daniel Russell, Letitia Anne Peplau

We will not dwell on depression and loneliness for a long time, but rather move on to a more interesting topic such as self-esteem:
- The Rosenberg self-esteem scale (RSES)—Morris Rosenberg
- The Rathus Assertiveness Scale (RAS)—Spencer Rathus
- The Interpersonal Diagnosis of Personality—Timothy Leary

Of course, this is not a complete list of all psychological diagnostic techniques. It should be noted that they were mainly developed in the 50-70th years of the last century. These are basic researches, tested by time and have not lost their relevance. Despite that the questionnaires are easy to carry out (question / answer, pictures), they can contain questions incomprehensible by the standards of modern mentality and be laborious in interpretation.

In child psychology, it is effective to use drawing tests and developmental techniques.
Drawing—projective tests are aimed at studying the mental state and personality traits, individual typological differences and ideas about one's family.
For example:
- The House-Tree-Person Test (HTP)—John Buck

- The Draw-a-Person test (DAP)—Florence Goodenough
- The Baum test (Tree test or Koch test)—Charles Koch
- The Kinetic Family Drawing (KFD)—Burns and Kaufman

To study the level of readiness of children for school, psychologists mainly use methodology designed to check logical thinking:
- The Raven's Progressive Matrices (RPM)—John Raven

Additionally, it is necessary to take into account techniques for the development and assessment of thinking, attention, memory, imagination and speech functions.

There are many IQ tests. Their choice depends on age and individual abilities and personal preferences.

One of the topics in the learning process is the comfort and psychological health of students.
This will help you figure it out:
- The School Anxiety Scale (SAS)—Beeman Phillips

This questionnaire will allow research, anxiety at school, the experience of social stress, fear of self-expression, situations of knowledge testing, fear of not meeting the expectations of others, problems with teachers, and more. There is also a scale for detecting general anxiety:
- The Children's Manifest Anxiety Scale aged 8-12 (CMAS)—A. Castaneda, B. McCandless, D. Palermo

It is important to measure the child's current ability and track developmental dynamics based on age.

These tests are recommended to be carried out using leading questions and choosing tasks that are suitable for your child. Do not impose those tests that are difficult and not understandable or if he simply does not want to carry them out.

The regime of self-isolation, restrictions with their constantly changing rules, influence of the virus and the pandemic as a whole strongly affect the social relation between people and in the family. We suggest to familiarize with a number of techniques aimed at studying interpersonal relationships:

- The Rosenzweig Picture Frustration Test (PFT)—Saul Rosenzweig, (child or adult versions), with shows the level of personality conflict and emotional response to social situations.
- The Sacks Sentence Completion Test (SSCT)—Joseph Sacks, Sidney Levy, allow you to be deep in thought on some questions (for example: family, work, gender relations) and develop, based on the analysis, an emotionally qualitative attitude to social and personal life. This is a very flexible and effective technique that you can create yourself. For children, make up your unfinished sentences, topics of which you are interested in (about school, parents, friends).

Reveals the atmosphere of family relationships and parenting methods from the point of view of the child:
- Children's Reports of Parental Behavior an Inventory (CRPBI)—E.S. Schaefer

From the point of view of the parent:
- Parent Attitude Research Instrument (PARI)—E.S. Schaefer, R.Q. Bell

As the last item from this list, we would like to indicate the actual system based on a graphical display of the distance between you and your environment. Its purpose is to identify the influence of various factors on increasing or decreasing the distance:
- The Comfortable Interpersonal Distance Scale (CIDS)—Stephen Nowicki, Jr., Marshall P. Duke

In the basic version, the authors suggest using a schematic representation in the form of circles and vectors. You can create any improvisation (ladder, multi-storey building, table with chairs, etc.). It will cheer you up and bring clarity to your interpersonal relationships.

In conclusion, we emphasize that in psychology there is no universal diagnostic method, which would reflect the full completeness of personality characteristic.

However, we made a thematic review of methods for identifying various psychological problems.

Remind you that these are professional psychological techniques that at home cannot serve for a full

examination without the participation of a certified specialist.
The purpose of this section was only to point out possible psychological problems for further study if necessary.

Recommendations of exit from quarantine

In a critical situation, several stages of adaptation are distinguished to solve emerging psychological problems.

The first stage is awareness. In the world, there was an ambiguous position of society on the pandemic. The displayed carelessness, the inability of many people to believe in the seriousness of the situation in a short time led to a discussion among psychologists of the topic of awareness.

The modern establishment, corporate culture, fashion for beauty ideals, plastic surgery, have taught people to be overly demanding on their appearance and directly or indirectly played a negative role in quarantine.

The first awareness of society was to be wearing masks / protective gear and social distancing. In many countries, people, owing to their mentality, do not maintain personal distance. It seems very strange that smoking was not considered as a factor in the spread of infection by airborne droplets. In fact, here you can list a huge number of illogical actions that defy rational thinking.

For psychologists, this is a direct signal indicating big

problems in the psychology of consciousness.

It is necessary to realize that everyone should observe the regime of self-isolation and be protected by many rights—including health and the comfort of a hostel.

The second stage is the stage of acceptance. You need to find the positive in those measures that have become the norm, try to take them for granted without internal resistance. In fact, limitations are more likely to be constantly present with us in a strong or weak form. The pandemic has an undulating course, so you need to be prepared for recurring events. It would be extremely wrong if people ignore earlier mistakes in the future.

Third stage—choose a mode of action. Quarantine is for our safety, and compliance is our responsibility. Restrictive measures have reduced business activity, but this does not mean inaction; it is the most effective action for the benefit of all.

Since the goal is to preserve the life and health of people, it is very logical to perceive quarantine as a single working process of a responsible team. From this position, one can consider the negative trend of statements—that the regime of self-isolation is loneliness, as a delusion.

To develop a way to respond to a changed situation, you need to follow the rules and laws, consider your psychological capabilities and follow our recommendations.

Learn to reduce the level of anxiety—this will help you: a positive attitude, switching attention, breathing exercises, relaxing techniques.

In relation to children, it is necessary to increase their sense of confidence and independence. Organize fun activities and teach children to analyze what is happening. Let them be themselves—exaggerated demands reduce self-esteem and mood. Show attention and care.

Antistress program—despite the free schedule in quarantine, you should not drastically change the daily routine and diet. This is not the time to experiment, take risks, or seek extremes.

Pharmacologists note a sharp demand for antidepressants during the period of isolation. You should not self-medicate; these are potent chemicals that have many side effects, including addiction, and can only be prescribed by a psychiatrist.

Excessive consumption of alcohol, tobacco and other potent substances should also be avoided as a stress reduction. It has been proven that these funds only temporarily have a calming effect; with prolonged use, an increase in dependence occurs, a depression appears, which increases anxiety and irritation.

Avoid negative contacts and put off things that are unpleasant for you.

Choose pleasant calm music, movies and books with a proven script without shocking episodes.

Move more, use elements of reflexology, herbal medicine, massage techniques.

For many, auto-training is suitable—self-hypnosis, before going to bed, repeat the affirmative phrase several times that you and your family are safe. Draw a beautiful landscape in your mind, close your eyes.

Do not put off until tomorrow things that can be done today, so that they do not torment you before going to bed, and vice versa, transfer complex long projects, breaking their implementation into several phases so that there is no rush and excitement.

Find resources that increase the adaptive personality traits, new motivation to move forward.

Psychological formula:

High level of adaptation + Positive motivation

=

Low levels of anxiety and stress.

We hope that our book will clarify the basic psychological aspects and help to use new knowledge in real life.

The topics covered were considered from different positions of modern man and society. Psychology always strives to study the personality and answer the question: Who am I?!

The answer does not have to be quick, straightforward or short. Most often, people experience many different psychological states. It is important to learn how to measure, regulate emotions and not go beyond social behavior. Try to find comfort, considering the needs of other people.

The quarantine triggered a general recession in all sectors of life: economy, tourism, manufacturing, education, healthcare, and so on.

Society has always been alarmed by uncertain prospects, but now, thanks to scientific developments, a positive shift is outlined. The psychological state of people directly depends on economic factors, social security and culture.

In the light of the near future, psychologists should pay attention to the relationship between modern technology and humans. Artificial intelligence, robotics, is starting to compete with humans. This is comparable to the discovery of a new world. Created moral norms and rules of behavior are actively discussed in society. We hope that scientific and technological progress will change our lives for the better with reasonable minimum risks.

We wish you all the best!